Smocking Ideas

Smocking Ideas

Fiona Roediger

Kangaroo Press

Acknowledgments

Putting together a book like this cannot be undertaken alone so, for the help, support and encouragement of a number of people I give my sincere thanks:

• Tim and Kelly, two wonderful children who gladly helped without too much fuss, I love you dearly.
• Louise, a great sister who told me I could actually do it.
• Bev, a fabulous sister-in-law who helped when needed.
• Julie, Josie and Michelle, for their continuing support and encouragement. Everyone needs friends like these.
• Jae Fitzgerald, Ghia Spangenberg, Gemma Cameron, Zoe Stewart, Melissa and Desiree Mason and last but not least Kelly Roediger, seven gorgeous models who did their job on the day to perfection.
• Jill Parker and her fabulous staff at 'The Studio', Tony Carey Photographers of Port Lincoln, plus a big thank-you for the wonderful photography and the use of the 'Print Show'. Your encouragement on the day kept me awake.
• Polly, a great mother-in-law, who bought my pleater. Without you I would never have got so far.
• David at Kangaroo Press and his staff, a big thank you for encouraging me to do this.
• And last but by no means least my husband Ken, just for putting up with it all. You can now have the lounge room back to normal.

Reprinted 1996
First published in 1993 by Kangaroo Press Pty Ltd
3 Whitehall Road Kenthurst NSW 2156 Australia
P.O. Box 6125 Dural Delivery Centre NSW 2158
Printed in Hong Kong through Colorcraft Ltd

ISBN 0 86417 508 6

Contents

Foreword

This book is specifically designed for those who love the look of smocking but have always thought it would be too hard. I have taught smocking for a number of years, and often been asked for simple smocking designs—so this book is for you.

The stitches in this book—cables, waves and trellises—are all relatively simple and straightforward. The designs putting the stitches together are also quite straightforward, although they give results which look most satisfyingly complex.

I have included designs for garments, and for gifts, covering a wide selection of items—a bodice dress, a drop-waisted dress, baby's rompers, towels and coathangers, for example. So be inspired— happy smocking!

Introduction

Smocking is a traditional form of embroidery, in which the embroidery stitches are worked over the top of fine pleats. Smocking as we know it today originated in the rural areas of England in the late eighteenth century, when protective smocks were worn over ordinary working clothes. Smocking the front and back of the garment gave it extra fullness as well as adding extra warmth for protection against cold winds and rain. Besides giving warmth and protection, these farmers' garments also had to be hard wearing, practical and comfortable.

Until recently the only way to prepare fabric for smocking was to pleat it by hand using transfer dots, the tedious method our mothers and grandmothers used. Fortunately for those of us who enjoy smocking, pleating machines which take the agony out of the pleating process are now readily available. Many haberdashery shops have a pleater in store—they generally charge by the number of pleats—or you may have a friend with a pleater who will, for a small fee, pleat your fabric for you.

Smocking may look hard, but it is really very easy, and with only a handful of stitches you will soon be on your way to making the most beautiful clothes and gifts.

Materials and equipment

Fabric

We all want our finished garments to be worn and much loved by their wearers. When selecting fabric, remember not only colour, washability and texture, but the wearer's personality.

If you are a beginner choose simple open prints with one solid main colour, or a plain fabric. It is much easier to follow a smocking design on such a fabric. Cotton blend fabrics give the best results, as they tend to keep their shape better than other fabrics and wash well. Try crushing a piece of fabric in your hand before you buy it—if it creases very easily it will need a fair amount of ironing.

Choose the fabric and garment design to suit the wearer; a drop-waisted dress looks good on a taller or slimmer girl, but it does not suit a smaller child.

Once a piece of fabric is smocked it is reduced to one-third of its original width, so if your finished article needs to be 20 cm wide you will need a 60 cm width of fabric after selvages have been removed.

Needles

Select a needle that will push through your fabric with ease, with an eye large enough for easy threading. A No. 7 or No. 8 crewel is usually suitable. Keep a spare needle in your handbag to try in the fabrics you are considering buying; that way you can buy extra needles to suit a particular fabric, if necessary.

Thread

Embroidery threads are available in a wide variety of colours and types, but I find I use DMC No. 8 Perle Cotton most of the time. It comes in a ball and doesn't become twisted and knotted like most of the stranded cottons. It keeps very tidy, and there is no wastage from throwing away unwanted strands. If you prefer to use stranded cotton, however, use three strands of thread. As most stranded cottons have more than the three strands required they will have to be divided.

If you are smocking a child's dress from selvage to selvage, you will need to work with a one-metre length of thread. This will allow you to work across the pleated fabric without running out of thread, thus avoiding knots on the inside which tend to look untidy.

When selecting thread for a smocking project choose a shade darker than your fabric rather than lighter—a darker shade will stand out more. Always write down the number and colour of the thread that you have selected. I keep a special notebook with a page for each project I do; I attach to the page a piece of the fabric and small lengths of each thread I have used, identified by the type and colour number. This helps later on with colour coordination. I find this book invaluable when I buy thread, as there are always so many colours to choose from.

A design can change simply by changing the colour of one thread; the whole effect can be altered this way, which makes smocking interesting. It is really up to your own imagination. You will be amazed at how creative you can be—but be warned, fabric and craft shops may become irresistible!

Added touches

To finish off a smocked garment and add a professional look when I am attaching smocking or inserting it into a garment, I use satin piping (which can be bought from most haberdashery stores) or lace. This also helps to stabilise the pleats. Satin piping highlights the smocked work (if you spend all that time on smocking, you want to make sure people notice your lovely needlework!) and is not particularly expensive. Adding embroidered roses around collars and cuffs or around necklines looks pretty and can really dress up a garment. If it suits the particular garment, wide satin ribbons sewn into the side seams, to be tied into bows, can add extra sparkle. The embroidered cotton collars available at most haberdashery shops suit some fabrics better. You will be surprised how many simple, attractive ideas for finishing touches you will find when you look around—and experiment with your own special skills as well—you might surprise yourself with how original and artistic you can be.

General rules for smocking

1. All stitches in this book are worked from left to right.
2. For upward stitches the thread is kept below the needle.
3. For downward stitches the thread is kept above the needle.
4. For cable stitches the thread may be either above or below the needle, depending on which direction the next stitch takes.
5. After making each stitch give the thread a gentle tug to keep the tension even and give consistency to the stitches.
6. If the thread frays or becomes difficult to work with, tie it off and begin with a new thread.
7. If you need to start a new thread halfway through a row, bring the needle up next to the stitch just completed and push it through the pleat on the left (stitch just completed).
8. Do not cut a panel of smocking without machine stitching the line of the cut first. If you need to cut out armholes, mark where they need to go and then sew two or three lines of straight stitch with your sewing machine. Smocking cut without doing this will all come undone like knitting.
9. Use the gathering threads as guidelines to keep your smocking stitches straight.
10. Spend a little time when you start checking the first row of stitches for mistakes.
11. Keep your needle horizontal as you work, parallel to the gathering thread.

Starting and finishing

To start a row
To start a row, thread the needle and knot one end of the embroidery thread. Working from left to right, count three pleats across, and bring your needle from the back, between the third and fourth pleats, through to the right side. Now insert your needle into the third pleat. As you work each pleat pick up half the depth of the pleat. Your needle will be inserted from the right side of each pleat through to the left side (a form of back stitching). The needle is held horizontal, parallel to the gathering thread. Finish three pleats in from the other side also; this gives enough fabric for a flat surface for a seam.

To finish a row
To end a row, try to finish with a cable stitch if possible. Insert the needle into the valley between the last two pleats, taking it through to the back of the work. Pick up a little of the pleat and make a loop, pass the needle through the loop to make a tiny knot. Do this two or three times to make it secure.

Holding rows
When working smocking the first row and the last row of gathering are not smocked on—these two rows are called holding rows. These rows stabilise the pleats and keep them even, which makes the smocking easier to manage.

Stitches

Outline stitch—diagram 1
This is a very simple stitch to do, as the thread is always kept *above* the needle. Keeping the needle level with the gathering thread, pick up the first pleat ready for stitching—remembering to keep the thread above the needle. Use your thumb to help keep it there. Now continue to pick up each pleat till the end of the row.

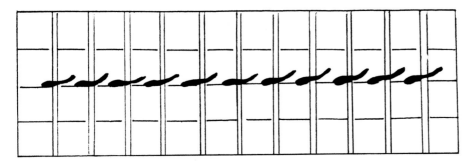

Diagram 1—Outline stitch

Stem stitch—diagram 2
This is the same stitch as the outline stitch, only this time the thread is kept *below* the needle. Again, use your thumb to help keep the thread in place.

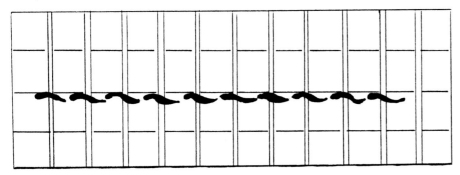

Diagram 2—Stem stitch

Wheat stitch—diagram 3
Wheat stitch combines outline stitch and stem stitch, worked on the same line with the outline stitch above the gathering thread and the stem stitch directly below the gathering thread. This forms an 'ear of wheat' effect. This combined stitch, which is very effective and really does look like wheat, works well on plain fabrics and fabrics with a simple pattern.

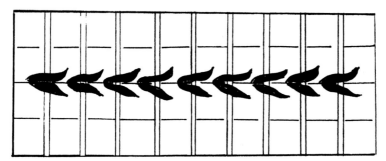

Diagram 3—Wheat stitch

Cable stitch—diagram 4

Cable stitch is the foundation for most smocking stitches. In cable stitch the thread is alternately above and below the needle. The needle never changes position, only the thread. Remember to keep the needle parallel to the gathering thread.

For a *bottom* or *under cable* the thread is below/under the needle.
For an *above* or *top cable* the thread is above/over the needle.

These are two of the most important rules for smocking.
 Cable stitch is a good stitch for backsmocking.

⌣ = thread under needle
⌢ = thread over needle

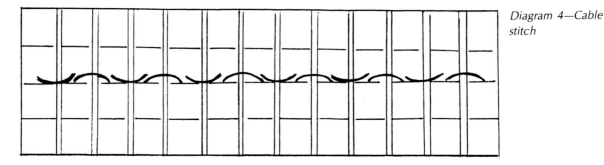

Diagram 4—Cable stitch

Double cable stitch—diagram 5

Work one row of cable across the pleats, alternating the thread above and below the needle. Start with an under cable. Now work another row of cable directly underneath the first row, so that the stitches touch each other. Start with an over cable.

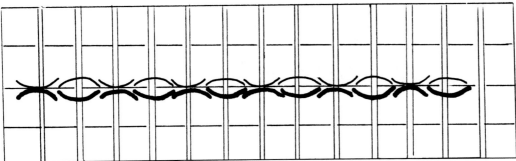

Diagram 5—Double cable stitch

Alternating cable stitch—diagram 6

Alternating cable stitch is lovely when done in two colours. It is a little difficult to do at first, but the end result is worth it.

Starting with a bottom cable, work one row of cable stitches—this is our base row. Now start a new row directly below the first row of stitches. Starting with a top cable, work three cables to the third cable (insert your needle diagonally from the right side of the pleat under the row above, pointing it upwards, and bring it out on the left side of the same pleat). Now do the next three cables *above* the base row. Before completing the third pleat insert the needle diagonally downward to come out underneath the first row of cable stitches.

Now you are ready to do the next three-cable sequence. This may seem a little hard at first, but persevere with it—in the end you will be glad that you did.

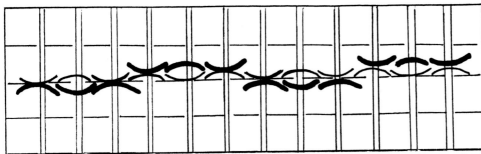

Diagram 6—Alternating cable stitch

Cable flowers—diagram 7

Work three cables (under-over-under), then directly below work another three cables (over-under-over). This looks lovely as a fill-in for diamonds.

13

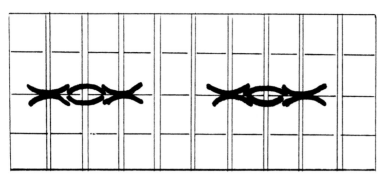

Diagram 7—Cable flowers

Trellis stitches—diagrams 8, 9 and 10
With this stitch you work up and down between the gathering threads. It is often referred to as zig-zag stitch.

All trellises start and finish with a cable stitch.

It is most important to remember:

> When going *up* the thread is *below* the needle.
> When going *down* the thread is *above* the needle
> For *bottom cables* the thread is *below* the needle.
> For *top cables* the thread is *above* the needle.

Whether going up or down the needle is still held horizontally and inserted into each pleat horizontally to the gathering thread, pointing back to the beginning of the work.

A cable stitch is used at the top and bottom of each zig-zag, and determines the direction of the next stitch.

A mistake is very easy to undo—just unthread the needle and gently push the needle's eye under the thread to make it come out.

Trellis stitches are worked in 'steps' of 2,3,4 or more. The number of steps indicates how many stitches there are between the top and bottom cables. Decide before you start how many steps are required. If it's four steps, then space them at the one-quarter, one-half and three-quarter marks between the rows.

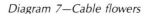

gathering thread
¾
½
¼
gathering thread

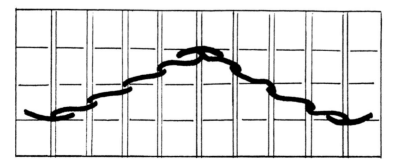

Diagram 8—Four-step trellis stitch

Start as you normally would, picking up the first pleat between halfway and the bottom gathering thread, picking up the next pleat at the halfway mark, then picking up the next pleat between the halfway mark and the top gathering thread. Pick up the fourth pleat and do a top cable above the line. Remember to change thread position—thread above the needle for a top cable.

As you move on to the next pleat, pick it up between the top gathering thread and the halfway mark, then pick up the next pleat at the halfway mark, the next pleat between the halfway mark and the bottom gathering thread. When you have completed the third stitch, do a bottom cable, remembering to change thread position.

As you come down with the trellis stitch it helps to keep the needle level with the upward stitch at that same level. Use your needle eye to help put stitches in the correct position.

These are the instructions for a three-step trellis; a two-step, four-step or five-step trellis is worked in exactly the same way—the only different is the number of steps. You can work another row of trellis stitches directly below the row just completed (see diagram 10).

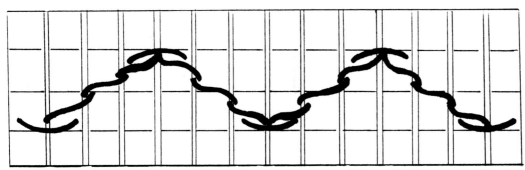

Diagram 9—Three-step trellis stitch

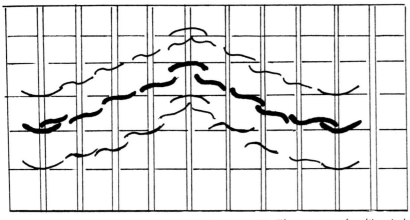

Diagram 10—Three rows of trellis stitch

Trellis diamonds—diagram 11
Reverse the trellis stitch to make a large diamond (see diagram 11). This can be done with various numbers of steps, but always use the same number below as above.

The possibilities with trellis stitch are endless—try a few ideas of your own. I like to do rows and rows of trellis stitch in different colours.

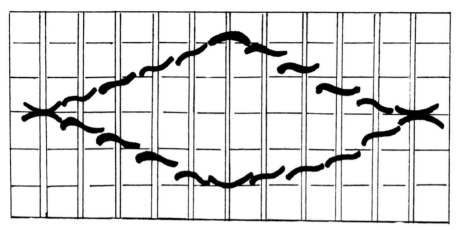

Diagram 11—Trellis diamonds

Wave stitch—diagrams 12 and 13
Wave stitch is one of my favourite stitches, and it combines well with other stitches. Wave stitch is worked between the rows of gathering threads.

Start in the usual way and do a bottom cable. With the thread below the needle follow the next pleat up to the gathering thread above, and pick it up. A top cable can now be done on the next pleat, remembering to change thread position. Follow the next pleat down to the bottom gathering thread and pick it up; now pick up the next pleat and do a cable for the bottom, remembering to change thread position.

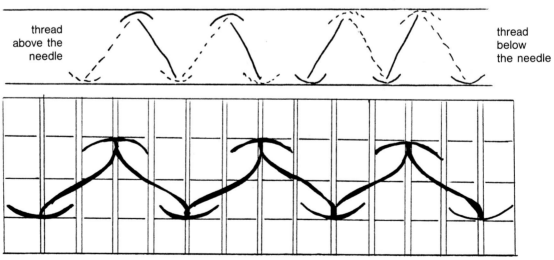

Diagram 12—Wave stitch

Try starting at the same spot and reversing the stitches to form a small diamond shape (see diagram 13).

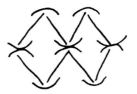

Diagram 13—Wave diamonds

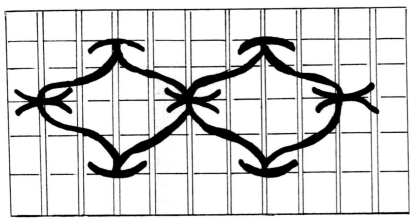

Cable and wave combinations—diagrams 14 and 15
These stitches follow the same principle as the wave, the only difference being in the cables at the top and bottom. Try your own combinations of stitches and colours of thread. You will be amazed at the number of choices you have—the huge variety of combinations.

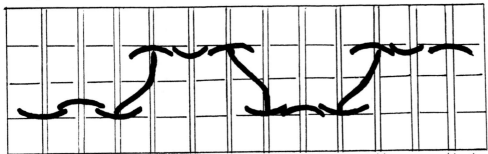

Diagram 14—Cable-wave combination

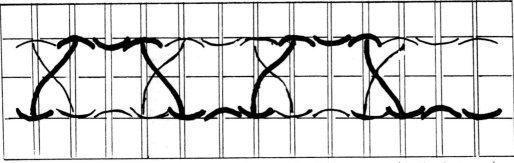

Diagram 15—Cable-wave combination in two colours

These stitches are the basis for all the projects covered in this book.

Many books already available describe many more stitches, but these are the most commonly used. Happy smocking—it is never too late to learn!

Melissa

The fabric used in this dress is a pure cotton, the first piece of material to catch my eye when I walked into the fabric shop. It cost a little more than I would usually pay for fabric, but I liked the feel and the look of it. Remember that a good quality fabric will look better and last longer than a cheap fabric, so buy the best you can afford that will suit the wearer.

I chose to smock this dress using only one thread colour (the same colour as the flowers), to enhance the tiny delicate flowers in the fabric.

I added three pearl buttons at the centre collar, satin piping on the front bodice, and cotton lace at the sleeve edges.

Instructions

Pleat 20 full-space rows.

Row 1: Do not smock—this is a holding row.
Row 2: Double cable.
Row 3: Outline and stem stitches, the two stitches combined making wheat stitch.
Rows 4 to 19 are all worked in a 3-step trellis.

Row 4: Work row 4 down to row 5.
Row 5: Work row 5 up to row 4.
Row 6: Work row 6 up to row 5, then down to row 7.
Row 7: Work row 7 up to row 6.
Row 8: Work row 8 up to row 7, then down to row 9.
Row 9: Work row 9 up to row 8.
Row 10: Work row 10 up to row 9, then down to row 11.
Row 11: Work row 11 up to row 10.
Row 12: Work row 12 up to row 11, then down to row 13.
Row 13: Work row 13 up to row 12.
Row 14: Work row 14 up to row 13, then down to row 15.
Row 15: Work row 15 up to row 14.
Row 16: Work row 16 up to row 15, then down to row 17.
Row 17: Work row 17 up to row 16.
Row 18: Work row 18 up to row 17, then down to row 19.
Row 19: Work row 19 up to row 18.
Row 20: Do not smock—holding row.

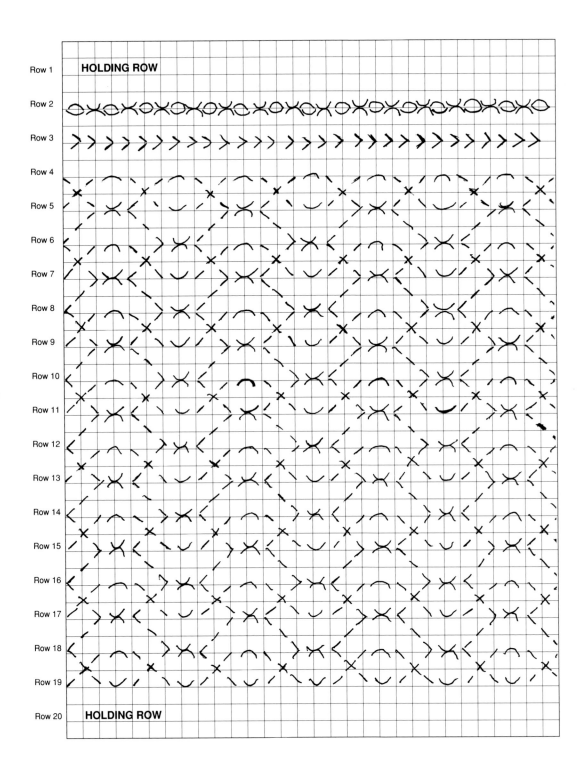

Row 1   **HOLDING ROW**

Row 2

Row 3

Row 4

Row 5

Row 6

Row 7

Row 8

Row 9

Row 10

Row 11

Row 12

Row 13

Row 14

Row 15

Row 16

Row 17

Row 18

Row 19

Row 20   **HOLDING ROW**

Blue drop-waisted dress

This dress was made for an older child (ten years and older).

I used the background colour of a dark apricot for the main smocking colour, and the background blue for the second (contrast) colour.

This dress is a drop-waisted style, and because of this I added pintucks in the middle of the bodice and on the shoulders.

I attached pre-gathered cotton embroidered lace around the neckline instead of a collar, and the same lace to edge the sleeves.

Instructions

Pleat 17 half-space rows.

Work rows 3 through to 16 using a 5-cable wave combination.

Rows 4 up to 3, 8 down to 9, 11 up to 10 and 15 down to 16 are all done with the contrast colour.

Row 1: Do not smock—holding row.
Row 2: Work row 2 using a cable stitch with the main colour.

Row 3: Work row 3 down to row 4, using the 5-cable wave combination. Use main colour.
Row 4: Work row 4 up to row 3, using contrast colour.
Row 6: Work row 6 up to row 5, using main colour.
Row 6: Work row 6 down to row 7, using main colour.
Row 8: Work row 8 down to row 9, using contrast colour.
Row 9: Work row 9 up to row 8, using main colour.
Row 10: Work row 10 down to row 11, using main colour.
Row 11: Work row 11 up to row 10, using contrast colour.
Row 13: Work row 13 up to row 12, using main colour.
Row 13: Work row 13 down to row 14, using main colour.
Row 15: Work row 15 down to row 16, using contrast colour.
Row 16: Work row 16 up to row 15, using main colour.
Row 17: Do not smock—holding row.

Row 1 **HOLDING ROW**

Row 2

Row 3

Row 4

Row 5

Row 6

Row 7

Row 8

Row 9

Row 10

Row 11

Row 12

Row 13

Row 14

Row 15

Row 16

Row 17 **HOLDING ROW**

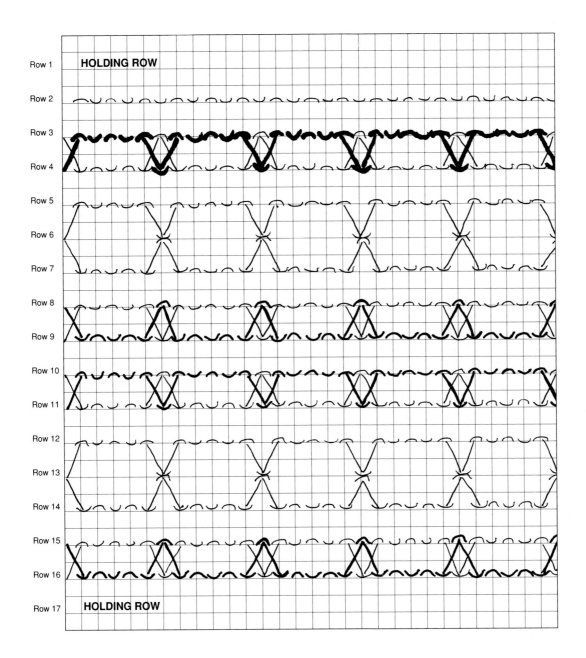

Ribbons and bows

This dress, made about six years ago, was one of the first dresses I ever made—and it still looks as good as new. Smocking doesn't date, it just looks better.

I chose a fabric with a simple pattern, so I could clearly see the results of my smocking efforts. I attached satin piping to the collar and bodice, and wide satin ribbon bows to the side seams. I wanted my daughter to be able to wear the dress for a few years so I added wide cotton lace to the hem and sleeves. I also added wide pleats to the sleeves between the cuff and the elbow, which could be let down for extra length. I used two contrast colours in the smocking for extra effect.

Instructions

Pleat 19 full-space rows.

Row 1: Do not smock—holding row.
Row 2: A single row of cable stitch.
Row 3: A single row of cable stitch in a second colour.
Row 4: A single row of cable stitch.
Row 6: Work row 6 up to row 5 with a full space wave stitch.
Row 5: Work row 5 down to row 6 with a crossover full space wave stitch (use second colour thread).
Row 7: Work row 7 up to row 6 with a 4-step trellis.
Row 7½: Worked upwards with a 4-step trellis.
Row 8: Work row 8 upwards with a 4-step trellis.

Row 8: Start at row 8 and work down to row 9 with a 3-cable wave combination.
Row 9: Work row 9 down to row 10 with a crossover 3-cable wave combination in a second colour.
Row 10: Work row 10 up to row 9 with a 3-cable wave combination.
Row 10: Work row 10 down to row 11 with a 3-cable wave combination.
Row 11: Work row 11 down to row 12 with a crossover 3-cable wave combination in a third colour.
Row 12: Work row 12 up to row 11 with a 3-cable wave combination.
Row 12: Work row 12 down to row 13 with a 3-cable wave combination.
Row 13: Work row 13 down to row 14 with a crossover 3-cable wave combination in the third colour.
Row 14: Work row 14 up to row 13 with a 3-cable wave combination.
Row 14: Work row 14 down to row 15 in a 3-cable wave combination.
Row 15: Work row 15 down to row 16 with a crossover 3-cable wave combination in the second colour.
Row 16: Work row 16 up to row 15 with a 3-cable wave combination.
Row 16: Work row 16 down to row 17 with the same 3-cable wave combination.
Row 18: Work row 18 up to row 17 with the 3-cable wave combination.
Row 19: Do not smock—holding row.

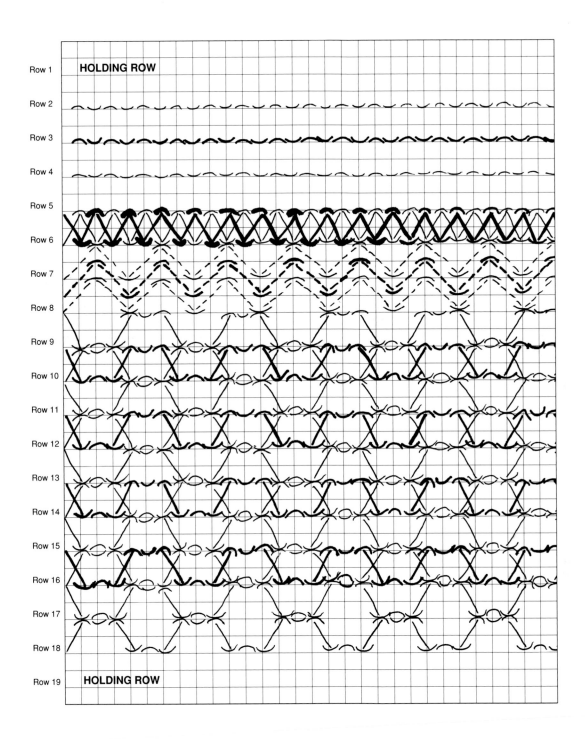

Row 1   **HOLDING ROW**

Row 2

Row 3

Row 4

Row 5

Row 6

Row 7

Row 8

Row 9

Row 10

Row 11

Row 12

Row 13

Row 14

Row 15

Row 16

Row 17

Row 18

Row 19   **HOLDING ROW**

23

Apricot delight

When I constructed this dress, I used satin piping and gathered lace around the collar, and satin piping on the bodice. I added apricot coloured satin ribbon at the waist as well as waist ties. The apricot ribbon, which has been tied into bows, highlights the delicate colours in the fabric. I also added broderie anglaise at the hem and sleeves, which apart from adding an enormous amount of length to the hems gives the finished garment a light and delicate look.

Instructions

Pleat 22 full-space rows.

Row 1: Do not smock—holding row.
Row 2: Cable stitch.
Row 3: Cable and alternating cable stitch.
Rows 4 through to 21 are all worked in a 3-step trellis.
Row 4: Work row 4 down to row 5 using main colour.
Row 5: Work row 5 up to row 4 and down to row 6 using contrast colour.
Row 6: Work row 6 up to row 5 and down to row 7 using main colour.
Row 7: Work row 7 up to row 6 using contrast colour, then row 7 down to row 8 using main colour.

Row 8: Work row 8 down to row 9 using main colour.
Row 9: Work row 9 down to row 10 using main colour.
Row 10: Work row 10 up to row 9 and down to row 11 using main colour.
Row 11: Work row 11 down to row 12 using main colour.
Row 12: Work row 12 down to row 13 using main colour.
Row 13: Work row 13 up to row 12 and down to row 14 using main colour.
Row 14: Work row 14 down to row 15 using main colour.
Row 15: Work row 15 up to row 14 and down to row 16 using main colour.
Row 16: Work row 16 down to row 17 using main colour.
Row 17: Work row 17 up to row 16 and down to row 18 using main colour.
Row 18: Work row 18 down to row 19 using contrast colour.
Row 19: Work row 19 up to row 18 and down to row 20 using main colour.
Row 20: Work row 20 up to row 19 and down to row 21 using contrast colour.
Row 21: Work row 21 up to row 20 using main colour.
Row 22: Do not smock—holding row.

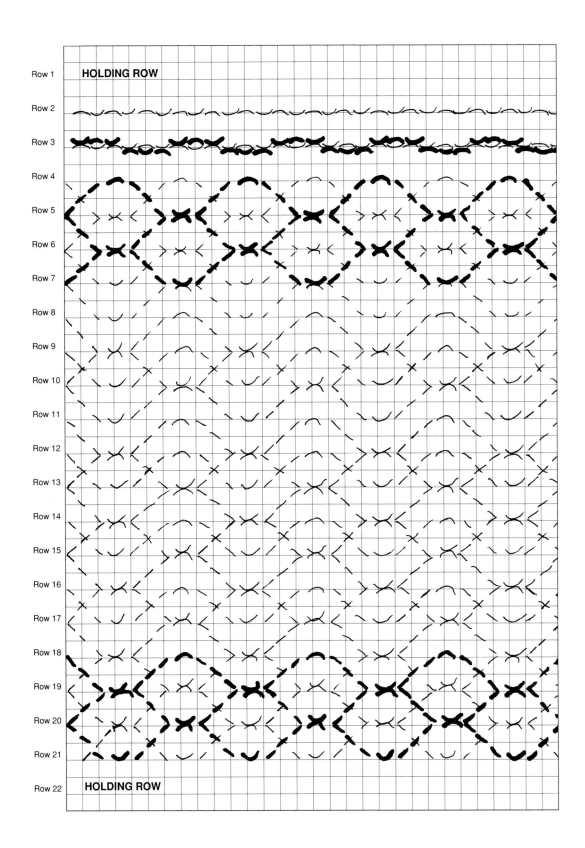

Row 1   **HOLDING ROW**

Row 2

Row 3

Row 4

Row 5

Row 6

Row 7

Row 8

Row 9

Row 10

Row 11

Row 12

Row 13

Row 14

Row 15

Row 16

Row 17

Row 18

Row 19

Row 20

Row 21

Row 22   **HOLDING ROW**

Ghia

Instructions

Pleat 15 full-space rows.

Row 1: Do not smock—holding row.
Row 2: Work a cable stitch to the end of the row.
Row 2½: Work row 2½ also with a cable stitch.
Row 3: Work row 3 down to row 4 with a 3-step trellis.
Row 4: Work row 4 up to row 3 and down to row 5 with a 3-step trellis.
Row 5: Work row 5 down to row 6 with a 3-step trellis.
Row 7: Back smock with a cable stitch.
Row 8: Work row 8 up to row 7 with 7 cables and a wave, and down to row 9 with 7 cables and a wave. Add roses in the centres of the open spaces.

Row 9: Back smock row 9 with a cable stitch.
Row 11: Work row 11 up to row 10 with a 3-step trellis.
Row 12: Work row 12 up to row 11 and down to row 13 with a 3-step trellis.
Row 13: Work row 13 up to row 12 with a 3-step trellis.
Row 14: Work row 14 up to row 13 with a 3-step trellis.
Row 15: Do not smock—holding row.

Add roses where required.

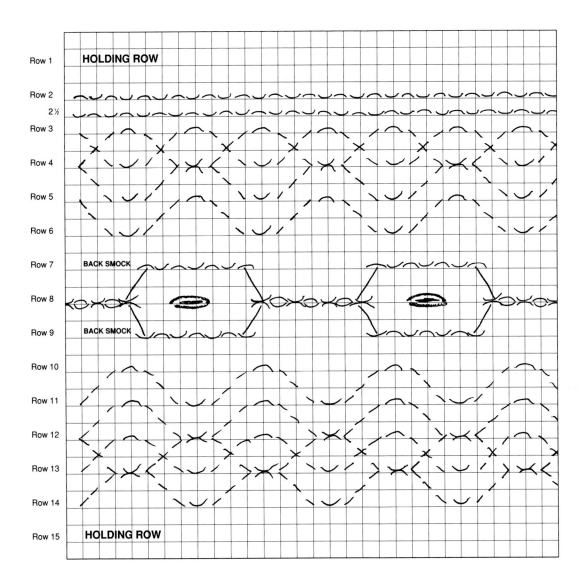

Row 1 — HOLDING ROW

Row 2
2½

Row 3

Row 4

Row 5

Row 6

Row 7 — BACK SMOCK

Row 8

Row 9 — BACK SMOCK

Row 10

Row 11

Row 12

Row 13

Row 14

Row 15 — HOLDING ROW

Triple delight

Instructions

Pleat 20 full-space rows.

Row 1: Do not smock—holding row.
Row 2: Work a single row of cable stitch with one colour, then work a row of alternating cable with a contrasting colour.
Row 2½: Work a single row of cable with a third colour.
Row 3: Work a row of cable stitch with the main colour, then work a row of alternating cable with a contrasting colour.
Row 3½: Work a single row of cable with a third colour.
Row 4: Work a row of cable with the main colour, then work a row of alternating cable with a contrasting colour.
Row 5: Start at row 5 and work down to row 6 with a 3-cable wave combination.
Row 6: Work row 6 up to row 5 with a cross-over 3-cable wave, using the second colour.
Row 7: Work row 7 up to row 6 with a 3-cable wave combination. Then work row 7 down to row 8 with a 3-cable wave combination.
Row 8: Work row 8 up to row 7 with a contrasting thread (either second or third colour) with a cross-over 3-cable wave combination.
Row 9: Work row 9 up to row 8 with a 3-cable wave combination, then work row 9 down to row 10 with a 3-cable wave combination.

Row 10: Work row 10 up to row 9 with a cross-over 3-cable wave combination, using contrasting thread.
Row 11: Work row 11 up to row 10 with a 3-cable wave combination, then work row 11 down to row 12 with a 3-cable wave combination.
Row 12: Work row 12 up to row 11 with a cross-over 3-cable wave combination, using a contrasting thread.
Row 13: Work row 13 up to row 12 with a 3-cable wave combination, then work row 13 down to row 14 with a 3-cable wave combination.
Row 14: Work row 14 up to row 13 with a cross-over 3-cable wave combination, changing the colour of the thread.
Row 15: Work row 15 up to row 14 with a 3-cable wave combination, then work row 15 down to row 16 with a 3-cable wave combination.
Row 16: Work row 16 up to row 15, changing the colour of the thread, with a cross-over 3-cable wave combination.
Row 17: Work row 17 up to row 16 with a 3-cable wave combination, then work row 17 down to row 18 with a 3-cable wave combination.
Row 18: Work row 18 up to row 17 with a cross-over 3-cable wave combination, changing thread colour.
Row 19: Work row 19 up to row 18 with a 3-cable wave combination.
Row 20: Do not smock—holding row.

Row 1   **HOLDING ROW**

Row 2
2 ½
Row 3
3 ½
Row 4

Row 5

Row 6

Row 7

Row 8

Row 9

Row 10

Row 11

Row 12

Row 13

Row 14

Row 15

Row 16

Row 17

Row 18

Row 19

Row 20   **HOLDING ROW**

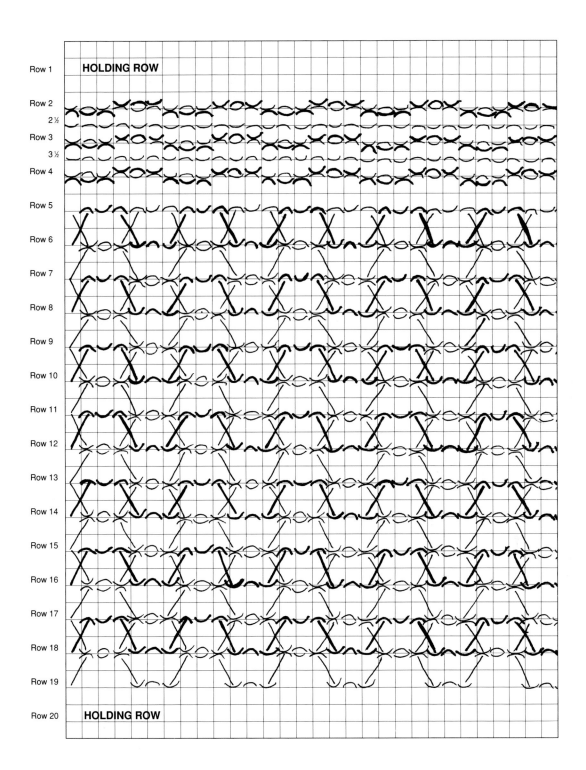

Mauve spring dress

The colours in this fabric reminded me of spring flowers ready to bloom. I chose smocking thread in colours to highlight the lacy delicate look of the fabric's flowers. I added satin piping to the smocking, and trimmed the collar with pre-gathered lace. I used the same lace on the sleeve edges.

Instructions

Pleat 16 full-space rows.

Row 1: Do not smock—holding row.
Row 2: Cable stitch.
Row 3: Cable and alternating cable stitch.
Row 4: Work row 4 up to row 3½ in a baby wave, and row 4 down to row 4½ in a baby wave.
Row 5: Cable and alternating cable.
Row 6: Backsmock this row to prevent pleats puffing out.

Row 7: Work a 4-step trellis up to row 6, then a 2-step trellis down to row 6½, a 2-step trellis up to row 6, and a 4-step trellis down to row 7. Continue in this pattern till the end of the row.
Row 8: Work row 8 upwards in the same pattern. Now reverse the pattern, working row 8 down to row 9.
Row 9: Work row 9 down to row 10 in the same pattern again. This will give an interesting pattern to which roses can be added in the middle of a double diamond.
Row 10: Backsmock (with a cable stitch).
Row 11: Cable and alternating cable stitch.
Row 12: Backsmock.
Rows 13, 13½, 14, 14½ and 15: Work all these rows in a 4-step trellis. Try a change of colour for added effect.
Row 16: Do not smock—holding row.

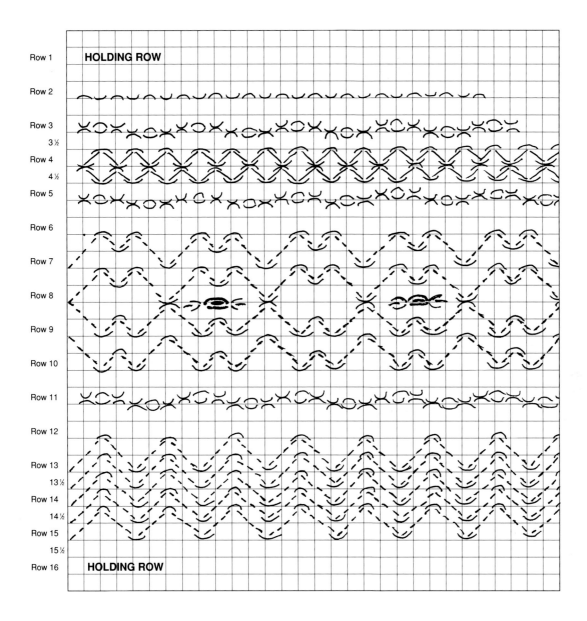

Row 1   **HOLDING ROW**

Row 2

Row 3

3 ½

Row 4

4 ½

Row 5

Row 6

Row 7

Row 8

Row 9

Row 10

Row 11

Row 12

Row 13

13 ½

Row 14

14 ½

Row 15

15 ½

Row 16   **HOLDING ROW**

Springtime party dress

This dress is a drop-waisted style suitable for older girls. Broderie anglaise added to the hem and sleeves highlights the smocking as well as the fabric.

Instructions

Pleat 12 full-space rows. Remember to pleat front and back of skirt.

Row 1: Do not smock—holding row.
Row 2: Cable stitch.
Row 3: Backsmock with a cable stitch.
Row 4: Work row 4 up to row 3 in a 4-step trellis.
Row 5: Work row 5 up to row 4 in a 4-step trellis.
Row 6: Work row 6 up to row 5 in a 4-step trellis.

Row 7: Work row 7 down to row 8 in a 4-step trellis.
Row 8: Work row 8 down to row 9 in a 4-step trellis.
Row 9: Work row 9 down to row 10 in a 4-step trellis.
Row 10: Work row 10 down to row 11 in a 4-step trellis.
Row 11: Work row 11 up to row 10 in a 4-step trellis.
Row 12: Do not smock—holding row.

Between rows 6 and 7 work roses in every second diamond, then backsmock with a cable stitch.

This design is also suitable for a bodice dress—just add a few more rows.

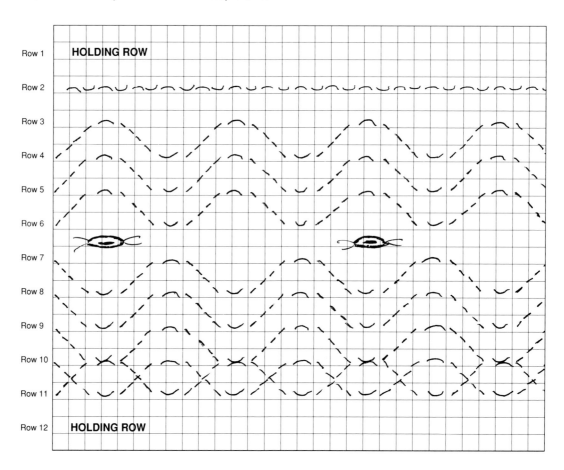

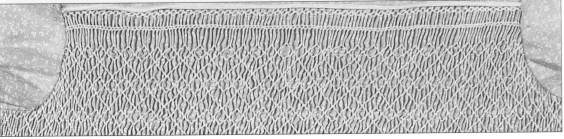

Melissa (see page 18)

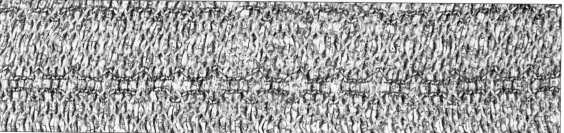

Blue drop-waisted dress (see page 20)

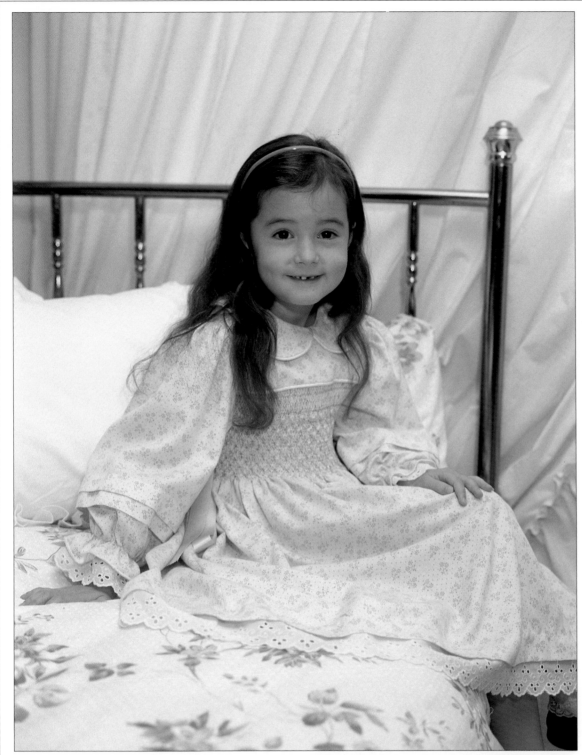

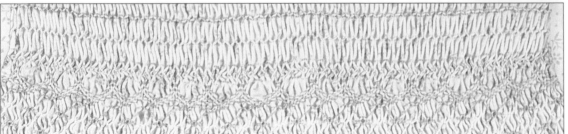

Ribbons and bows (see page 22)

Apricot delight (see page 24)

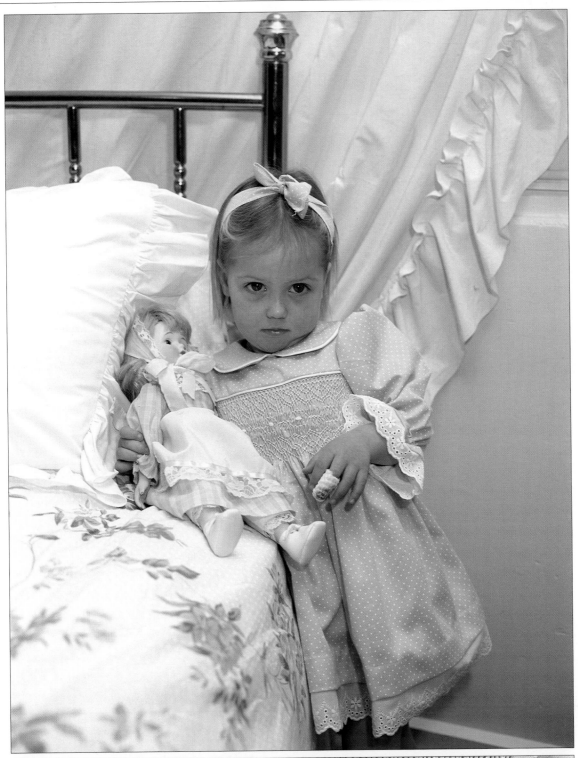

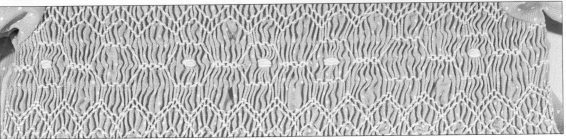

Ghia (see page 26)

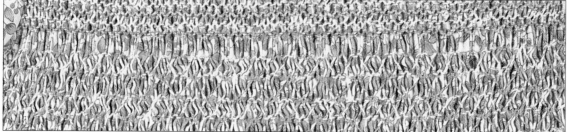

Triple delight (see page 28)

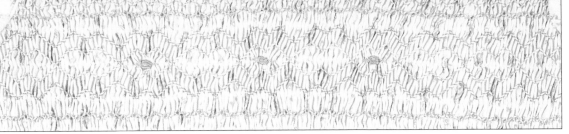

Mauve spring dress (see page 30)

Springtime party dress (see page 32)

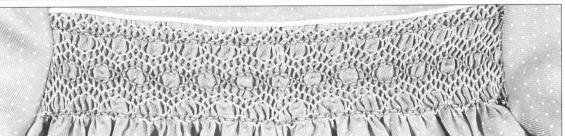

Blue rompers (see page 49)

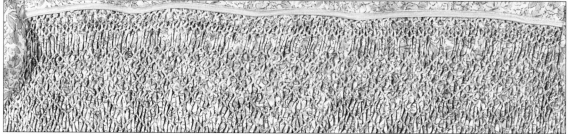

Fleur (see page 50)

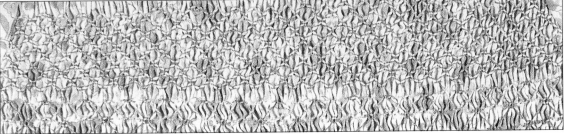

Blue shadows (see page 52)

Tartan rompers (see page 54)

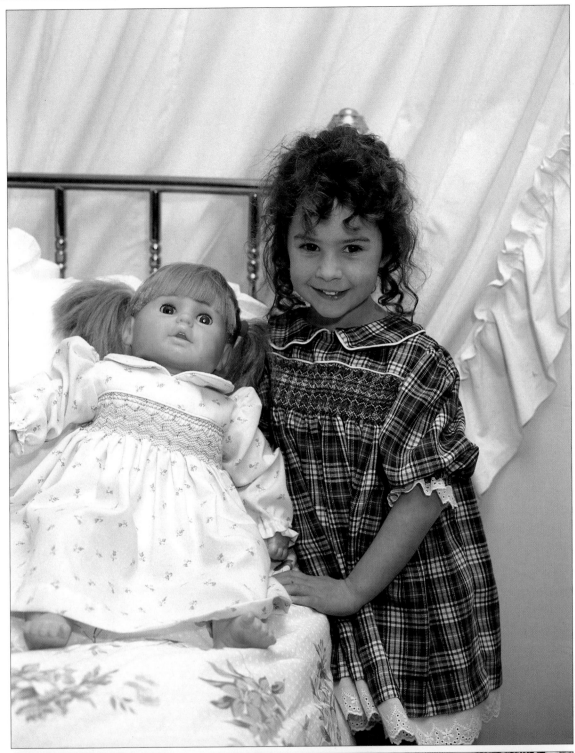

Tartan dress (see page 54)

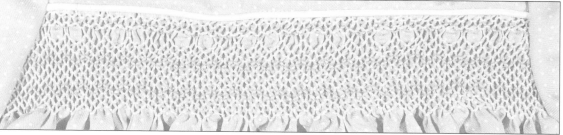

Baby waves (see page 55)

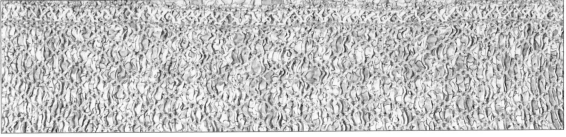

Liberty pink (see page 56)

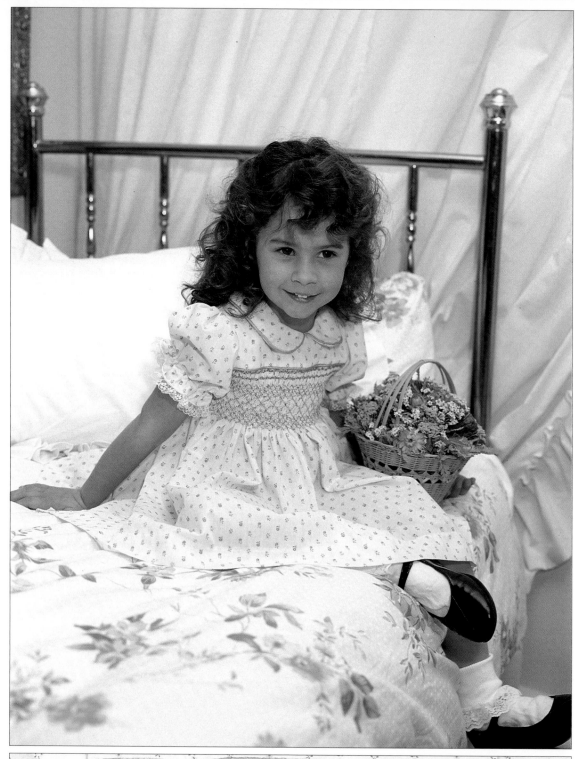

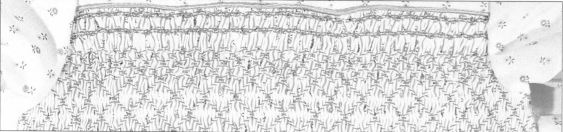

Jae (see page 57)

Blue rompers

Instructions

Pleat 7 half-space rows.

Row 1: Do not smock—holding row.
Row 1½: Work this row with a cable stitch.
Row 2: Work row 2 with a cable and alternating cable.
Row 3: Work row 3 up to row 2½ with a 2-step trellis.
Row 3½: Work row 3½ up to row 3 with a 2-step trellis.
Row 4: Work row 4 up to row 3½ with a 2-step trellis and down to row 4½ with a 2-step trellis.

Row 4½: Work row 4½ down to row 5 with a 2-step trellis.
Row 5: Work row 5 down to row 5½ with a 2-step trellis.
Row 6: Work row 6 with a cable and alternating cable stitch.
Row 7: Do not smock—holding row.

Because of the simplicity of this design you can work as many rows as desired, but for rompers this amount is ideal.

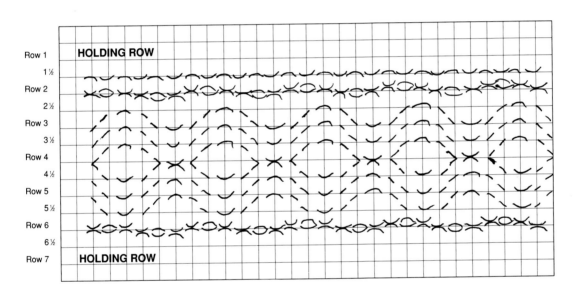

49

Fleur

Instructions

Pleat 15 full-space rows.

Row 1: Do not smock—holding row.
Row 2: Work row 2 in cable stitch, using contrast colour.
Row 2½: Work row 2½ in cable stitch, using main colour.
Row 3: Work row 3 in cable stitch, using contrast colour.
Rows 4 through to 14 are all worked in a 3-step trellis, using main and contrast colours.
Row 4: Work row 4 down to row 5 using main colour.
Row 5: Work rows 5 up to 4 and 5 down to 6 using contrast colour.

Row 6: Work rows 6 up to 5 and 6 down to 7 using main colour.
Row 7: Work row 7 up to row 6 using contrast colour.
Row 8: Work row 8 up to row 9 using main colour.
Row 9: Work row 9 up to row 10 using main colour.
Row 10: Work row 10 up to row 11 using main colour.
Row 11: Work row 11 up to row 10 and down to row 12 using main colour.
Row 12: Work row 12 up to row 11 and down to row 13 using contrast colour.
Row 13: Work row 13 up to row 12 and down to row 14 using main colour.
Row 14: Work row 14 up to row 13 using contrast colour.
Row 15: Do not smock—holding row.

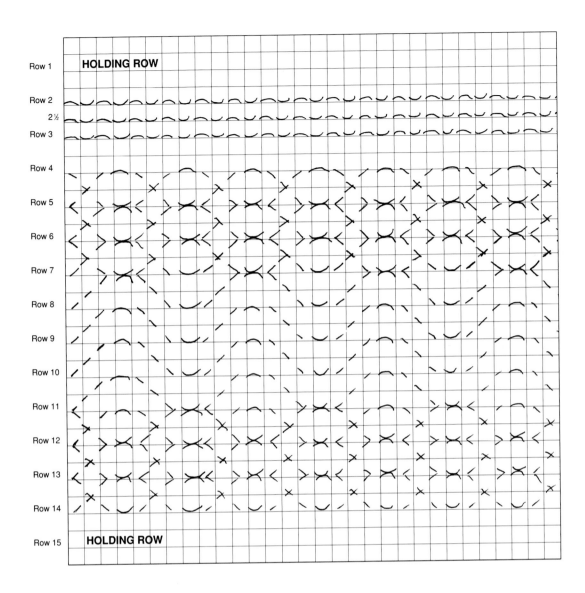

Row 1   **HOLDING ROW**

Row 2

2½

Row 3

Row 4

Row 5

Row 6

Row 7

Row 8

Row 9

Row 10

Row 11

Row 12

Row 13

Row 14

Row 15   **HOLDING ROW**

Blue shadows

This dress was made for an older girl who wanted the smocked look without it being too fussy. I found this particular piece of fabric interesting to work, with a variety of colour choices to use for smocking threads. I used three colours, but in no set order.

Satin piping and gathered lace trim the collar of this dress, keeping the hems deep to give the finished garment a more professional look.

Instructions

Pleat 20 full-space rows.

Row 1: Do not smock—holding row.
Row 2: Work row 2 with a cable stitch, using the main colour thread.
Row 3: Work row 3 with a cable and alternating cable stitch, using the main colour and a contrasting colour.
Row 4: Work row 4 down to row 5 with a 3-step trellis.
Row 5: Work row 5 up to row 4 with a cross-over 3-step trellis.
Row 6: Work row 6 up to row 5 with a cross-over 3-step trellis, and down to row 7 with the same cross-over 3-step trellis. Try adding a third colour.
Row 7: Work row 7 up to row 6 with a cross-over 3-step trellis, and down to row 8 with a cross-over 3-step trellis.
Row 8: Work row 8 up to row 7 with a cross-over 3-step trellis, and down to row 8½ with a baby wave. Use the main colour for this row.
Rows 9 through to 14 are all worked with a cross-over 3-cable wave combination. I used three different colours.

Row 9: Work row 9 down to row 10 with a 3-cable wave combination.
Row 10: Work row 10 up to row 9 with a cross-over 3-cable wave combination.
Row 11: Work row 11 up to row 10 with a cross-over 3-cable wave combination, and down to row 12 with a cross-over 3-cable wave combination.
Row 12: Work row 12 up to row 11 in a cross-over 3-cable wave combination, and down to row 13 in a cross-over 3-cable wave combination.
Row 13: Work row 13 up to row 12 with a cross-over 3-cable wave combination.
Row 14: Work row 14 up to row 13 with the same cross-over 3-cable wave combination.
Row 14½: Work row 14½ down to row 15 with a baby wave.
Row 15: Work row 15 down to row 16 in a 3-step trellis.
Row 16: Work row 16 up to row 15 in a cross-over 3-step trellis, and down to row 17 in a cross-over 3-step trellis.
Row 17: Work row 17 up to row 16 in the same 3-step cross-over trellis, and down to row 18 in a 3-step cross-over trellis.
Row 18: Work row 18 up to row 17 in a 3-step cross-over trellis, and down to row 19 in a 3-step cross-over trellis.
Row 19: Work row 19 up to row 18 in a 3-step cross-over trellis.
Row 20: Do not smock—holding row.

Row 1 · **HOLDING ROW**

Row 2

Row 3

Row 4

Row 5

Row 6

Row 7

Row 8

Row 9

Row 10

Row 11

Row 12

Row 13

Row 14

Row 15

Row 16

Row 17

Row 18

Row 19

Row 20 · **HOLDING ROW**

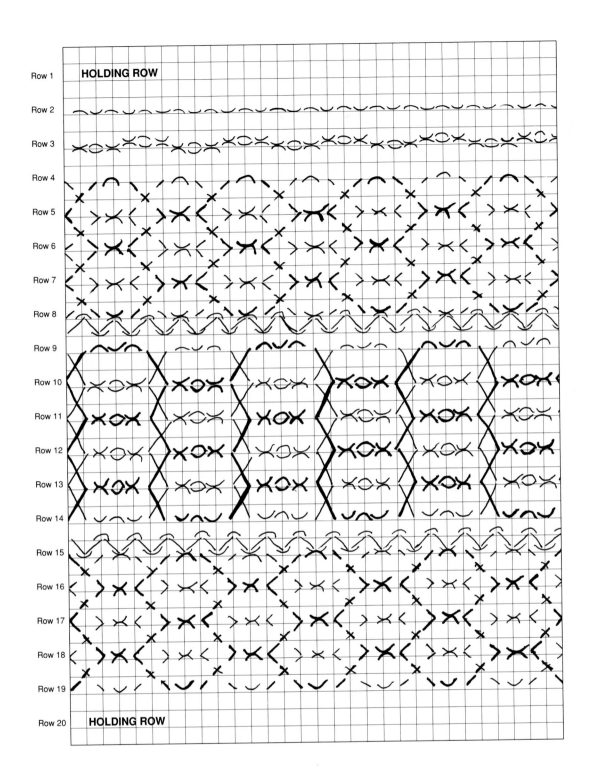

Tartan trellis

Here, because of the busy nature of the tartan, I have chosen the simplest of designs—a 2-step trellis all in the same direction, using only two colours, pure white and a strong red. This gives the effectiveness of smocking while highlighting the fabulous tartan.

Care must be taken when pleating tartan fabric as the pleating can become distorted very easily, or even look distorted. When preparing to pleat the tartan I lined up the first smocking row with one of the fine white lines woven into the pattern. This gave a good guide for the first row of smocking, and balanced with the tartan look once the pleated gathering threads were removed.

This particular smocking design is lovely on baby's garments, and is also fabulous when used on fabric of only one colour—for example, try white thread on pink or blue spotted fabric, or pink on a white baby's nighty.

Instructions

This design is pleated with half-space rows.

Row 1: Do not smock—holding row.
Row 1½: Cable and alternating cable.
Row 2½: Work from row 2½ up to row 2 in a 2-step trellis.
Row 3: Work up to row 2½ in a 2-step trellis.
Row 3½: Work up to row 3 in a 2-step trellis.

Repeat this pattern till you have as many rows as you require. Remember—do not smock the last row as it is a holding row.

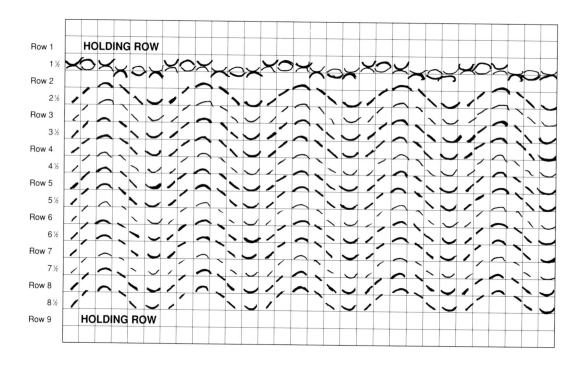

Baby waves

This is a charming design for a baby's first dress. It works very well on pink with a tiny white spot, a popular choice for baby girls. I used white thread for the main colour, and added a little pink to higlight this very simple and easy design. Try the baby waves dress for that special baby that you know. This design is also suitable for fabric with a tiny print, and for boy's and girl's rompers. Add more rows if you like.

Instructions

Pleat 7 half-space rows.

Row 1: Do not smock—holding row.
Row 1½: The first row is a single row of cable stitches.
Row 2: Cable and alternating cable.
Rows 2½ through to 6½ are all worked with a baby wave stitch.
Row 7: Do not smock—holding row.

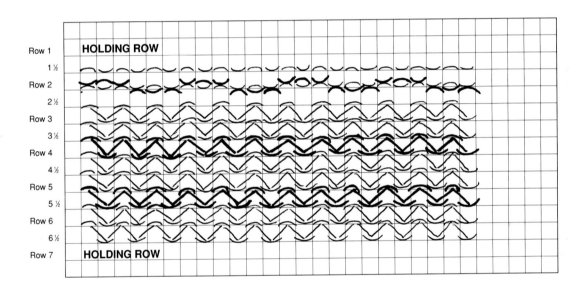

Liberty pink

Liberty fabric is very beautiful to look at and to work with, so I suggest you keep your design simple. It is also rather expensive, so work out carefully how much you will need. A drop-waisted girl's dress takes 2 metres of fabric. I added pintucks down the front bodice of the dress and cotton lace at the neck edge. I also added wide embroidered cotton lace at the sleeves and hem.

I chose to smock with only one colour, white, on the piece of Liberty fabric that I used; this suited my particular taste.

Instructions

Pleat 13 half-space rows.

Row 1: Do not smock—holding row.
Row 2: Row 2 is a single row of cable stitch.

Row 2½: Row 2½ is a wave stitch, with a cable stitch directly underneath the wave, then a row of 3 cables and a wave down to row 3.
Row 3½: Row 3½ is a 3-cable wave up to row 3. Then work row 3½ down to row 4 with the 3-cable wave combination.
Row 4½: Work row 4½ up to row 4 with a 3-cable wave combination, then work row 4½ down to row 5 with the 3-cable wave combination.
Row 5½: Work row 5½ up to row 5 with a 3-cable wave combination, then work row 5½ down to row 6 with the 3-cable wave combination.
Row 6½: Work row 6½ up to row 6 with a 3-cable wave combination, then work row 6½ down to row 7 with a 3-cable wave combination.
Row 7½: Work row 7½ up to row 7 with the same 3-cable wave combination.
Row 8: Do not smock—holding row.

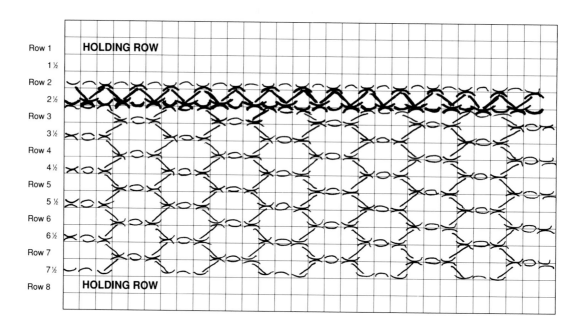

Jae

This design is suitable for a high-waisted dress, but can easily be adjusted for a deeper bodice.

The contrasting coloured diamonds at the top and bottom of the pattern bring out the colours in the fabric.

Instructions

Pleat 12 full-space rows.

Row 1: Do not smock—holding row.
Row 2: Work a single cable row with a main colour, then work an alternating cable with a contrasting colour.
Row 3: Same as row 2.

Row 4: Work row 4 down to row 5 with a 3-step trellis in the main colour.
Row 5: Work row 5 up to row 4 and down to row 6 with a 3-step trellis in the contrasting colour.
Row 6: Work row 6 up to row 5 and down to row 7 with a 3-step trellis in the main colour.
Row 8: Work row 8 up to row 7 and down to row 9 with a 3-step trellis in the main colour.
Row 9: Work row 9 down to row 10 with a 3-step trellis in the contrasting colour.
Row 10: Work row 10 up to row 9 and down to row 11 with a 3-step trellis in the main colour.
Row 11: Work row 11 up to row 10 with a 3-step trellis in the contrasting colour.
Row 12: Do not smock—holding row.

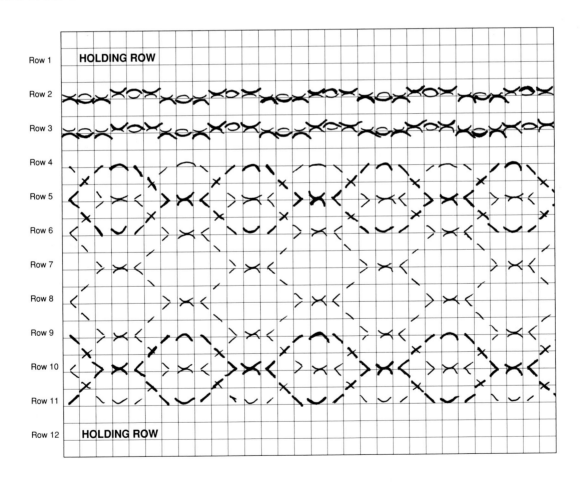

Coathanger 1

This smocked coathanger makes a lovely gift for someone special, and is very easy to do. (It also uses up left-over pieces of material.) You will need a length of fabric selvage to selvage, 16 cm deep. Cut the selvages off each end to prevent pleater needles bending and snapping.

Instructions

Pleat 14 full-space rows.

Row 1: Do not smock—holding row.
Row 2: Cable stitch.
Row 3: Cable stitch.
Row 4: Work row 4 down to row 5 in a cross-over 3-cable wave combination in a contrasting colour.
Row 5: Work row 5 up to row 4 and down to row 6 in a 3-cable wave combination.
Row 7: Work row 7 up to row 6 in a 3-cable wave combination.
Row 8: Work row 8 down to row 9 in a 3-cable wave combination.
Row 10: Work row 10 up to row 9 and down to row 11 in a 3-cable wave combination.
Row 11: Work row 11 up to row 10 in a cross-over 3-cable wave combination in a contrasting colour.
Row 12: Cable stitch.
Row 13: Cable stitch.
Row 14: Do not smock—holding row.

This design can be adapted, and looks just as nice if you leave out row 4 up to row 5 and row 11 up to row 10, which are the two rows using the contrast colour.

Construction

Remove the holding pleating threads and stretch out the completed work. Sew gathered lace just above the first row of cable stitching and just below the bottom row (where the two holding rows were).

Fold work in half lengthways (lace edges to meet). With right sides together sew the two ends together several times just inside all the knots. Cut off the excess on each side of the seam and turn in the right way. Find the centre point and make a tiny cut to allow the hook to go through.

Cover the coathanger with wadding or similar padding and oversew or glue in place. Place the smocked cover over the top, pushing the hook through the tiny hole. Neatly sew together underneath where the lace joins on to the fabric.

Cut a piece of gathered lace slightly longer than the hook and push it over the hook as a casing. Tie a ribbon around the base of the hook and glue down with craft glue. Glue around the top of the hook to prevent the lace fraying. Leave the coathanger to dry.

Now when you have made a pretty dress you can use the leftover fabric to make a matching coathanger.

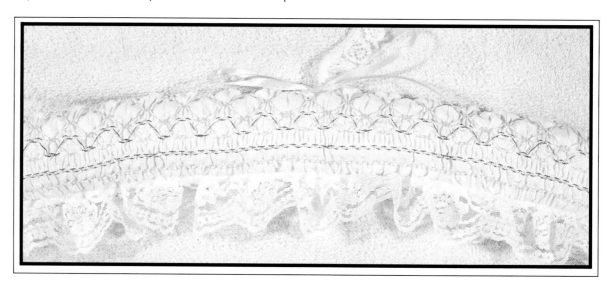

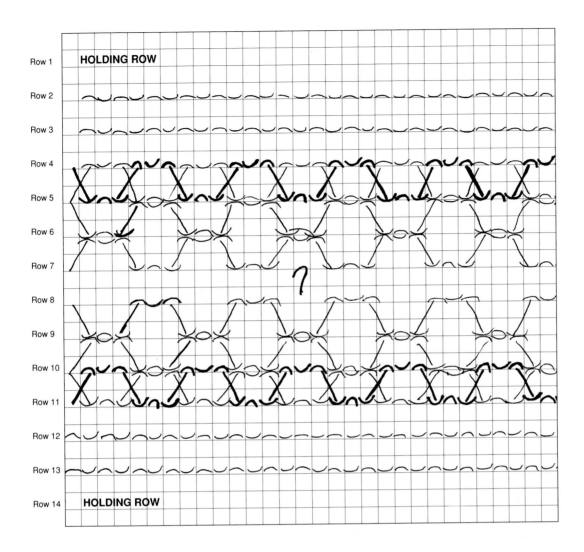

Coathanger 2

Although this design can be done using two or more colours, here I have used only one main colour. The design is based on a 3-step trellis, but more trellis steps can be added if you like. I have added embroidered roses in the middle of the trellis diamonds. The coathanger is constructed in the same way as the first one (see page 58), and the materials required are the same.

Instructions

Pleat 14 full-space rows, once again removing the selvages first.

Row 1: Do not smock—holding row.
Row 2: Cable stitch.

Row 3: Cable stitch.
Row 5: Work row 5 up to row 4 and down to row 6 with a 3-step trellis. This forms diamond shapes in which roses can be embroidered.
Row 7: Work row 7 up to row 6 with a 3-step trellis.
Row 8: Work row 8 down to row 9 with a 3-step trellis.
Row 10: Work row 10 up to row 9 and down to row 11 with a 3-step trellis.
Row 12: Cable stitch.
Row 13: Cable stitch.
Row 14: Do not smock—holding row.

Now work embroidered flowers in the diamonds and make up the coathanger.

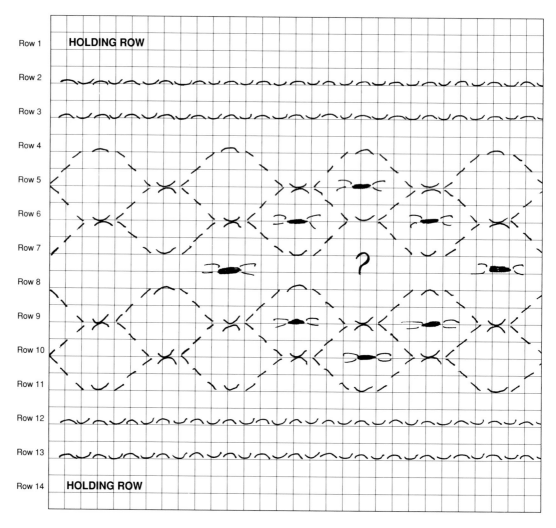

Apricot towel

Smocking on broderie anglaise is a lovely addition to a boring handtowel—it not only brightens your towel but also your bathroom. You can use any colour you like for the smocking. A smocked handtowel also makes a perfect gift for that person who is hard to buy for.

You will need a piece of broderie anglaise or eyelet lace three times the width of the towel you wish to sew it onto. It needs to be about 6 cm deep. If you have an overlocker, overlock the raw edge at the top, or stitch it with a tiny zigzag—this makes it easier to smock without a lot of little frayed bits getting in the way.

Care must be taken when pleating not to break the pleater needles with the pattern on the broderie anglaise.

Instructions

Pleat 8 to 10 half-space rows—the number will depend on the depth of the lace.

Row 1: Do not smock—holding row.
Row 1½: Work row 1½ with a cable stitch.
Row 2: Work row 2 down to row 2½ with a cross-over 3-cable wave combination.

Row 2½: Work row 2½ up to row 2 with a 3-cable wave combination, and down to row 3 with a 3-cable wave combination.
Row 3½: Work row 3½ up to row 3 with a 3-cable wave combination, and down to row 4 with the same 3-cable wave combination.
Row 4½: Work row 4½ up to row 4 with a 3-cable wave combination.
Row 5: Do not smock—holding row.

Construction

Remove holding threads and block smocked piece of lace to the desired width.

Place lace on towel and pin in position. Starting about 2.5 cm from the edge of the towel, sew along smocked lace piece to about 2.5 cm from the other edge of the towel. Thread ribbon through a length of insertion lace and pin it on top of the smocked piece, just a fraction above the first cable row of stitching. Sew in place along both the top and bottom edges of the insertion lace. Turn under raw edges at the sides of the towel and sew down neatly. Sewing can be done with hand or machine, but it must be done carefully so as not to show the stitching.

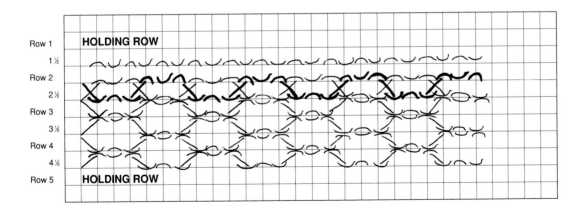

Pink towel

On this pink towel I chose to use a touch of soft grey with a dark rose pink thread.

Although the pattern is very similar to the one on the apricot towel I wanted to make a difference to the design using extra cables. This design has two more cables in between the baby waves, giving it a quite different look.

Instructions

Follow the pleating hints on page 61 and pleat 9 half-space rows.

Row 1: Do not smock—holding row.
Row 1½: Row 1½ is a single row of cable stitches, using the main colour.

Row 2: Row 2 is worked down to row 2½ with a 5-cable wave combination, using the contrast colour.
Row 2½: Row 2½ is worked down to row 3 with the same 5-cable wave combination, using the main colour.
Row 3: Row 3 is worked down to row 3½ with the 5-cable wave combination, using the main colour.
Row 4: Row 4 is worked up to row 3½ with the 5-cable wave combination, using the main colour.
Row 4½: Row 4½ is worked up to row 4 with the same 5-cable wave combination, using the main colour.
Row 5: Do not smock—holding row.

Work embroidered roses along row 3½.

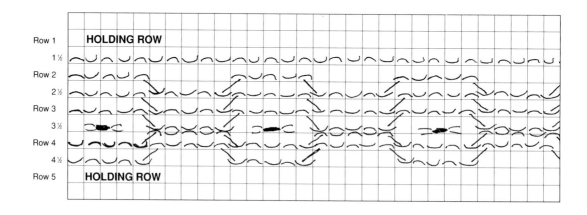

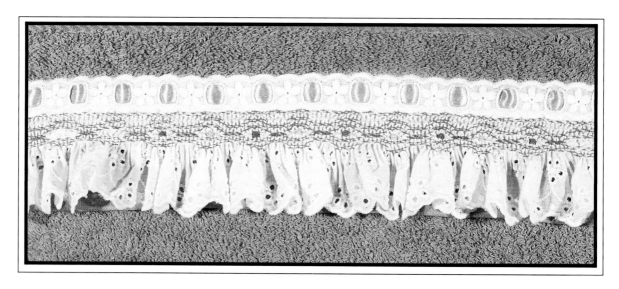

Bathroom curtain

Having had my small bathroom painted not long ago, I wanted new curtains that were 'different'—hence smocked curtains. I chose colours to complement the newly painted walls.

Smocked curtains with smocked handtowels and coathangers would be a lovely addition to any bathroom.

Measure the depth of the window and allow for hems. Multiply the final width of the curtain by three to calculate the width of fabric required. If the fabric will have to be joined to get the desired width, sew only a very tiny seam to allow the fabric to pass through the pleating machine. If you are using a fine fabric spray-starch it a few times before you iron it, and the fabric will roll through the pleater without the pleats popping out.

I hemmed the two sides and the bottom of the curtain, and made the casing for the curtain rod to go through, before I started smocking.

Instructions

Pleat 10 full-space rows.

Row 1: Do not smock—holding row.
Row 2: Work one row of cable stitch with your main colour choice, and a row of alternating cable with your second choice colour.
Row 3: Work row 3 the same as row 2.
Row 5: Start at row 5 and work up to row 4 with a 5-step trellis, do a top cable, then work down with a 2-step trellis, do a bottom cable, another 2-step trellis going up, a top cable and then a 5-step trellis. Repeat this pattern all along the row.
Rows 6 to 9: Repeat row 5 all the way through to row 9, alternating between the main colour and the contrast colour.
Row 10: Do not smock—holding row.

This can have more rows of smocking if you wish.

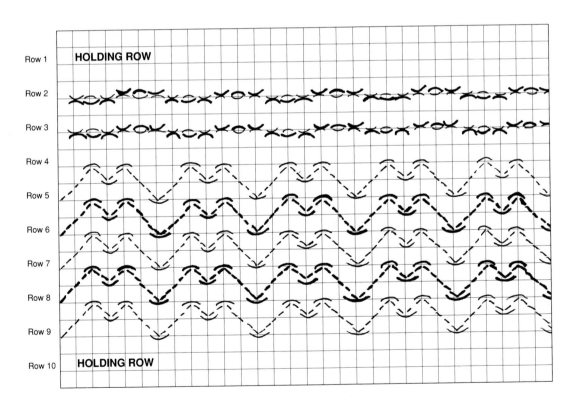

63

Index